INSIDE YOUR BODY

ALL

ABOUT

CUTS AND

BRUISES

FRANCESCA POTTS, RN

Consulting Editor, Diane Craig, MA/Reading Specialist

Super Sandcastle

An Imprint of Abdo Publishing
abdopublishing.com

ABDOPUBLISHING.COM

Published by Abdo Publishing, a division of ABDO, PO Box 398166, Minneapolis, Minnesota 55439. Copyright © 2018 by Abdo Consulting Group, Inc. International copyrights reserved in all countries. No part of this book may be reproduced in any form without written permission from the publisher. Super SandCastle™ is a trademark and logo of Abdo Publishing.

Printed in the United States of America,
North Mankato, Minnesota
062017
092017

Production: Mighty Media, Inc.
Editor: Liz Salzmann
Cover Photographs: Shutterstock
Interior Photographs: iStockphoto, Shutterstock

Publisher's Cataloging-in-Publication Data
Names: Potts, Francesca, author.
Title: All about cuts and bruises / by Francesca Potts, RN.
Description: Minneapolis, MN : Abdo Publishing, 2018. | Series: Inside your body
Identifiers: LCCN 2016962851 | ISBN 9781532111181 (lib. bdg.) | ISBN 9781680789034 (ebook)
Subjects: LCSH: Wounds and injuries--Juvenile literature. | Bruises--Juvenile literature.
Classification: DDC 617.1--dc23
LC record available at http://lccn.loc.gov/2016962851

Super SandCastle™ books are created by a team of professional educators, reading specialists, and content developers around five essential components—phonemic awareness, phonics, vocabulary, text comprehension, and fluency—to assist young readers as they develop reading skills and strategies and increase their general knowledge. All books are written, reviewed, and leveled for guided reading, early reading intervention, and Accelerated Reader™ programs for use in shared, guided, and independent reading and writing activities to support a balanced approach to literacy instruction.

CONTENTS

YOUR BODY — 4

ALL ABOUT YOUR SKIN — 6

TYPES OF SKIN INJURIES — 8

CAUSES OF SKIN INJURIES — 10

TREATMENT — 12

HEALING HELP — 14

WHEN TO SEE A DOCTOR — 16

HOW A BRUISE HEALS — 18

HOW A CUT HEALS — 20

PREVENTION — 22

GLOSSARY — 24

YOUR BODY

YOUR SKIN

You're amazing! So is your body.
Most of the time your body works just fine.
It lets you go to school, play with friends,
and more. But sometimes you feel sick or
part of you hurts.

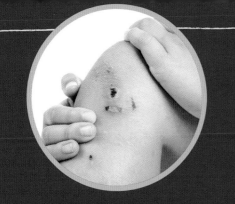

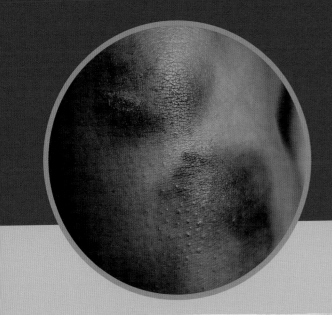

Cuts and bruises are two ways your body can get hurt. These are **injuries** to your skin. They can be painful. But these injuries are usually easy to treat.

ALL ABOUT YOUR SKIN

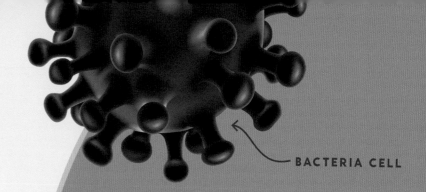

BACTERIA CELL

Your skin is your body's largest organ. It does many different things.

- It helps protect your body from bacteria.

- It protects your body from the sun's harmful rays.

- It helps your body's temperature stay normal.

- It gives you your sense of touch.

Your skin has three main layers. They are the epidermis, the dermis, and the hypodermis.

The epidermis is the top layer. It protects your body and makes new skin cells.

The dermis is under the epidermis. It is the thickest layer of skin. There is a lot going on in your dermis.

- It has **glands** that produce sweat and oil.

- It has **nerve** endings that give you your sense of touch.

- It is where your hair grows out of.

- It has blood vessels that supply your skin with blood. So, an **injury** to the dermis will bleed.

The hypodermis is the bottom layer. It is made up mostly of fat. This layer helps secure your skin to your muscles and bones. It also helps control your body's temperature.

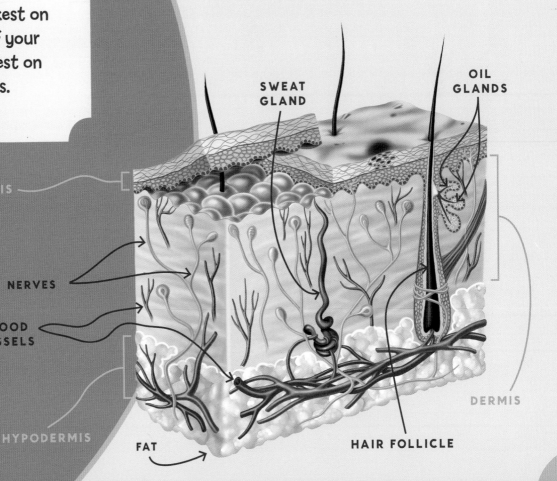

EPIDERMIS

NERVES

BLOOD VESSELS

HYPODERMIS

FAT

SWEAT GLAND

OIL GLANDS

DERMIS

HAIR FOLLICLE

TYPES
OF SKIN INJURIES

There are several common types of skin **injuries**. Sometimes two or more types occur together. For example, if you fall on the sidewalk, your knee could get a scrape and a bruise.

Cuts

A cut is a hole or tear in your skin. Cuts can be deep and bleed a lot.

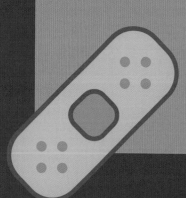

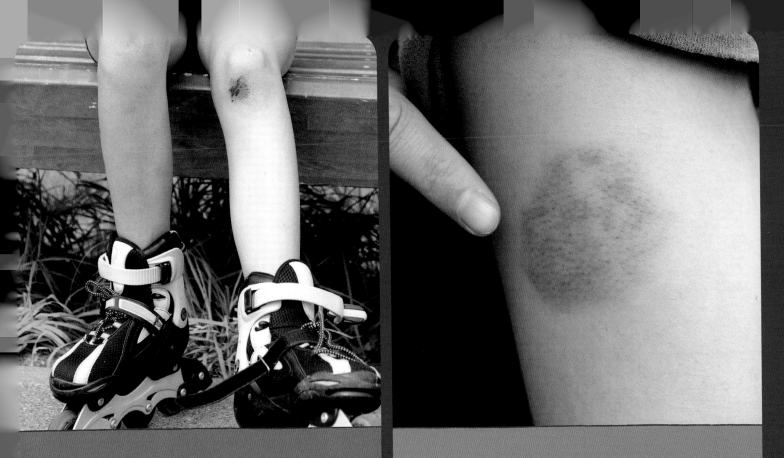

Scrapes

A scrape is when the top layer of skin gets rubbed off. It may or may not bleed. Knees, elbows, and palms are common places people get scrapes.

Bruises

A bruise happens when blood vessels under your skin break. Blood flows out of the broken blood vessels. This causes your skin to change color in that area.

CAUSES

OF SKIN INJURIES

Your skin can be **injured** in many ways. Often it happens while you are doing everyday activities.

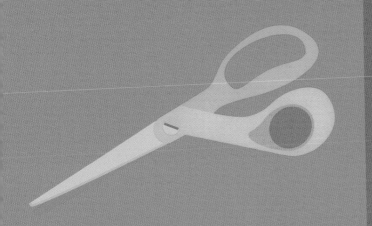

SHARP OBJECTS CAN CUT
YOUR SKIN.

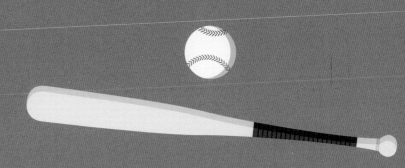

GETTING HIT BY A HARD
OBJECT CAN CAUSE A BRUISE.

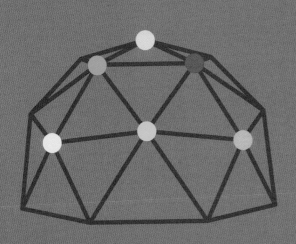

FALLING DOWN CAN CAUSE
SCRAPES AND BRUISES.

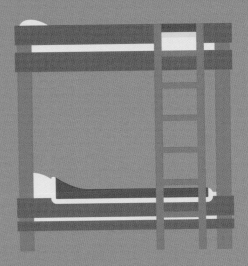

BUMPING INTO FURNITURE
CAN CAUSE BRUISES.

TREATMENT

M ost cuts and bruises are not serious. A parent, teacher, or another adult can treat them.

TREATING A CUT

Stop the Bleeding

Apply pressure to a cut to stop the bleeding. Press a clean cloth firmly over the cut. Keep pressing until the bleeding stops. This usually takes a few minutes.

Prevent Infection

Clean the cut thoroughly with soap and water. Pat the cut dry. Put **ointment** on the cut. Then cover the cut with a **bandage**. Change the bandage every day. It is important to keep the area clean.

TREATING A BRUISE

Cold Pack

Wrap a cold pack or bag of ice in a cloth. Hold it against the **injured** area. This can help reduce the size of the bruise. Ice can also help the bruise heal faster.

Elevation

Raise the bruised area above the level of your heart. This reduces the amount of blood flowing to the injured area. So, less blood can pool and form a bruise.

HEALING HELP

MEDICINES

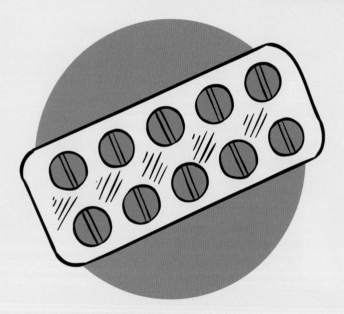

Acetaminophen and ibuprofen reduce pain from a cut or bruise.

An antibiotic **ointment** can keep a cut from getting **infected**.

NATURAL REMEDIES

Eat and drink foods with **vitamin** C. Vitamin C can speed up the growth of new skin cells.

Apply vitamin E **lotion** to the cut. Vitamin E can help the healing process and reduce scarring.

WHEN TO SEE
A DOCTOR

Most cuts and bruises don't need to be treated by a doctor. But some do. It is important to know when an **injury** needs a doctor's care. A large or deep cut may need to be sewn closed. This keeps dirt out of the cut.

See a doctor if a cut or scrape:

- doesn't stop bleeding

- is a deep cut near your chest, stomach, head, or neck

- has dirt in it that you can't wash out

- shows any signs of being **infected**

- causes severe pain that pain medicine doesn't relieve

See a doctor if a bruise:

- remains purplish, bluish, or blackish for longer than two weeks

- becomes increasingly swollen and painful

- causes you to be unable to move

- is near your eye and affects eye movement and vision

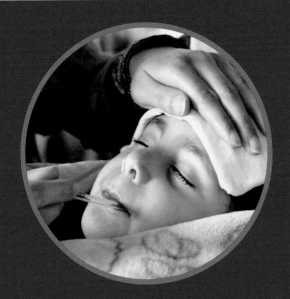

SIGNS A CUT IS INFECTED

- fever
- redness around the cut
- swelling around the cut
- **pus** coming out of the cut

HOW A BRUISE

HEALS

Everyone gets bruises sometimes. Bruises are very common **injuries**. They usually fade completely in about two weeks. During this time, bruises change color.

The Life of a Bruise

DAY OF INJURY

Redness appears on the surface of the skin.

DAYS 2 THROUGH 4

The redness turns purplish, bluish, or blackish. This is a sign of healing.

DAYS 5 THROUGH 10

The bruise grows more faint. It may turn greenish or yellowish.

DAY 11 AND AFTER

The bruise turns a light yellowish-brown color. It becomes lighter and lighter until it disappears.

HOW A CUT
HEALS

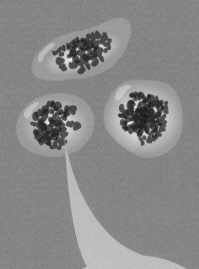

It takes one to two weeks for a cut to heal. The blood from the cut starts the healing process. Blood has special cells called platelets. The platelets in the blood near the cut stick together. They form a **clot** that seals the cut. When the clot dries, it forms a scab. The scab protects the area while new skin grows underneath it. Then the scab falls off.

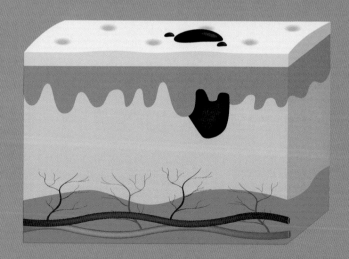

PLATELET
(*PLATE-lit*)

....

a type of blood
cell that helps
blood form clots

Will It Leave a Scar?

A scar is a mark left on the skin by a healed cut. Large cuts can leave more noticeable scars than small cuts. But there are ways to prevent or reduce scarring.

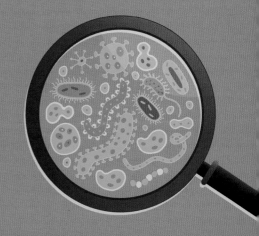

• Keep the cut covered while it heals so it stays clean.

• Don't pick at the scab. A scab can feel **itchy**, but try not to scratch it. Pulling the scab off might cause the cut to bleed again. Then a scar is more likely to form.

PREVENTION

It is important to remember that accidents happen! They are unexpected and hard to stop. But there are ways to protect your skin from **injury**.

Safety Gear

When playing sports, use safety gear. And wear long sleeves and pants. These will protect your skin if you fall.

Use Tools Properly

Craft and building projects can be a lot of fun. But some of them require sharp tools. Have an adult help you use these tools safely.

Kitchen Safety

Many cooking tools can cause skin **injuries**. Be careful when using them. Make sure an adult is nearby to help if needed.

GLOSSARY

BANDAGE - a covering that protects part of the body that has been hurt.

CLOT - a thick clump of blood.

GLAND - an organ in the body that makes chemicals that your body needs.

INFECTION - an unhealthy condition caused by bacteria or other germs. If something has an infection, it is infected.

INJURE - to cause pain or harm. An injured area is called an injury.

ITCHY - feeling irritated or bothersome.

LOTION - a thick liquid that is rubbed onto your skin.

NERVE - one of the threads in the body that takes messages to and from the brain.

OINTMENT - a smooth substance that is rubbed on the skin to help heal a wound or to reduce pain.

PUS - a thick, yellowish substance the body produces when it has an infection.

VITAMIN - a substance needed for good health, found naturally in plants and meats.